COLOUR WITH
CHRIS HUMFREY'S
AWESOME
AUSTRALIAN
ANIMALS

24 pages of colouring fun!

Shingleback
Tiliqua rugosa

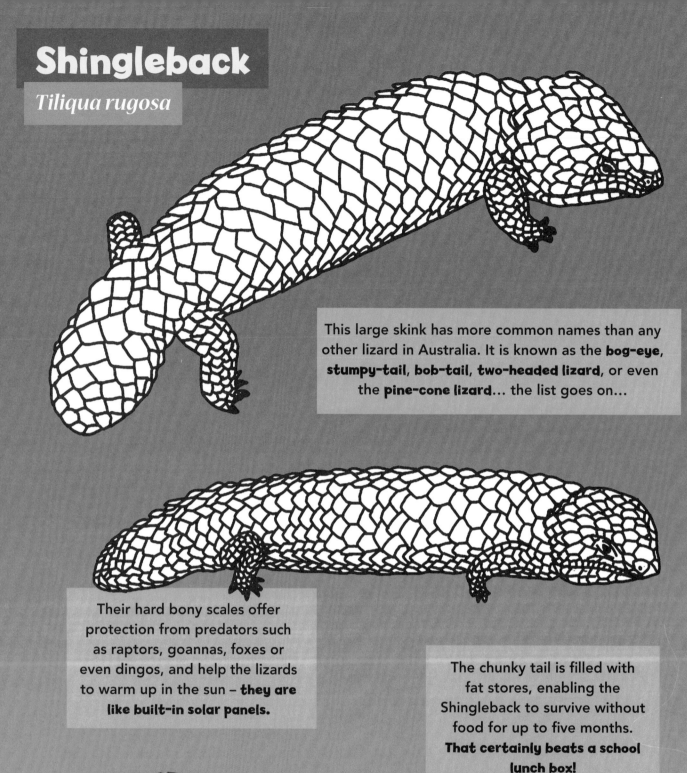

This large skink has more common names than any other lizard in Australia. It is known as the **bog-eye**, **stumpy-tail**, **bob-tail**, **two-headed lizard**, or even the **pine-cone lizard**... the list goes on...

Their hard bony scales offer protection from predators such as raptors, goannas, foxes or even dingos, and help the lizards to warm up in the sun – **they are like built-in solar panels.**

The chunky tail is filled with fat stores, enabling the Shingleback to survive without food for up to five months. **That certainly beats a school lunch box!**

SCAN HERE
to watch a WILD clip

azazer

Rough-throated Leaf-tailed Gecko

Saltuarius salebrosus

This large gecko spends most of its life clinging to cave walls or trees in Queensland's forests, perfectly camouflaged from predators and unsuspecting prey. It is **arboreal**, meaning 'tree loving,' and **nocturnal**, meaning 'mostly active at night'.

Juvenile

Leaf-tailed geckos can **change their colour** depending on their body temperature needs, becoming darker to absorb more heat from the sun's rays and warm up, or paler to reflect the sun's energy when they are too hot.

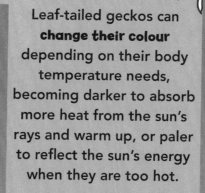

When this lizard grows larger, it sheds its skin like a dirty old sock. **That's much cheaper than buying clothes at the shop!**

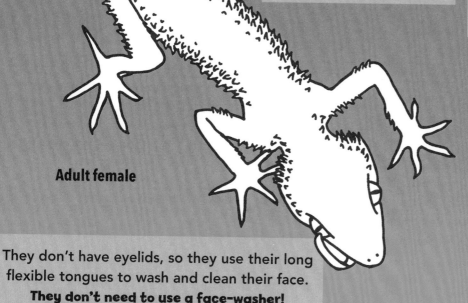

Adult female

They don't have eyelids, so they use their long flexible tongues to wash and clean their face. **They don't need to use a face-washer!**

SCAN HERE
to watch a WILD clip

exogof

If a predator grabs this gecko by the tail, they can drop their tail as a decoy and escape. This is called **autotomy**. The tail will grow back, albeit not as pretty or as detailed as the original one. A caudal lure on the tip of the tail is wriggled to attract small insect prey. Once an insect is enticed, this ambush predator deftly pounces on its unsuspecting dinner.

Lace Monitor
Varanus varius

The two-pronged tongue is used to 'sniff' out potential prey. **That is so COOL – they can smell in stereo!**

In southern parts of its range, this wonderful lizard is classified as **endangered**. Humans have destroyed Lace Monitor habitat for collection of firewood and land clearing for development and farming purposes.

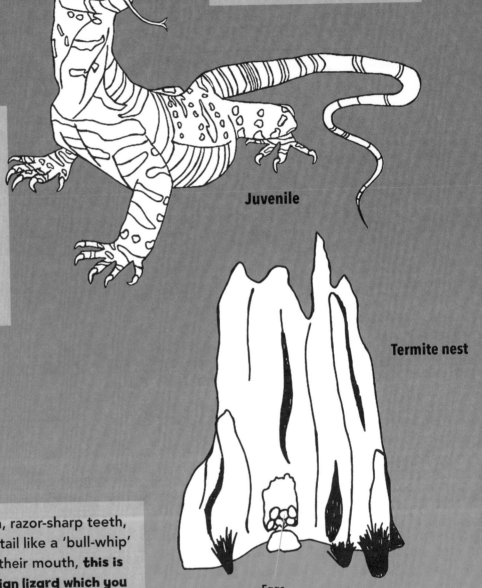

Juvenile

Termite nest

Eggs

Armed with tough skin, razor-sharp teeth, long powerful claws, a tail like a 'bull-whip' and necrotic saliva in their mouth, **this is definitely one Australian lizard which you don't want to mess with!**

These lizards are **HUGE!** Males grow larger than females, reaching just over 2 metres in length.

Adult female

Females deposit their eggs into termite mounds. Up to seven months later they return to free the newly hatched young... by digging them out. **Wow, that's one great MUM!**

SCAN HERE
to watch a WILD clip

ogatim

Jungle Carpet Python

Morelia spilota cheynei

Many people throughout the world understandably fear snakes, but once you get to know them you can't help but fall in love with them. **Snakes do such a great job for people. They eat up all of the mice and rats!**

This tree-loving denizen of Far North Queensland's tropical rainforests has the ability to eat huge prey items, many times larger than its own head. They can survive on just **10 meals a year**.

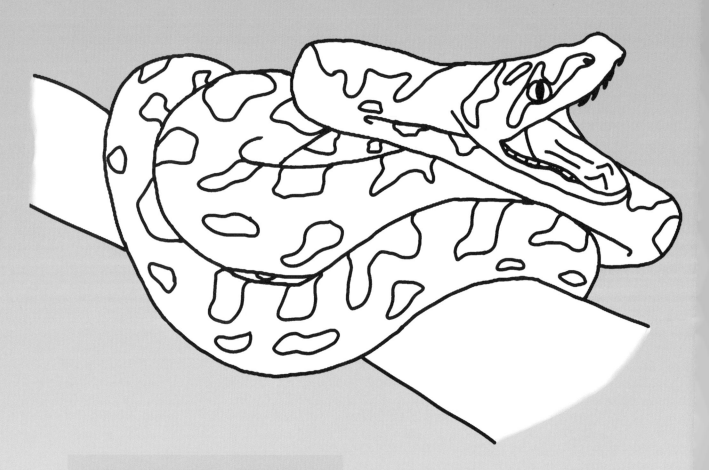

The lower jaw is not fused, instead it's held together by flexible muscles and ligaments. This enables the snake to **stretch its lower jaw out incredibly wide.**

Jungle Carpet Pythons have a muscular and flexible prehensile tail. They use it to grab on as they climb. **It's kind of like a hand... or a monkey's tail for hanging on.**

Jungle Carpet Pythons don't have to go to the shops to buy their clothes, when they grow larger, their old skin peels off, making a new shiny one underneath. **That's much cheaper and more eco-friendly than buying clothes.**

The female python **incubates** her eggs, protectively coiling around them. She 'shivers', vibrating her muscles to keep the eggs warm. The female will not eat during the 60 days of incubation. Once hatched, the babies have to fend for themselves.

SCAN HERE
to watch a WILD clip

uridun

Eastern Long-necked Turtle

Chelodina longicollis

Sometimes referred to as the 'stinker,' if disturbed or captured they are famous for emitting a noxious foul stench in an attempt to dissuade would-be predators from eating them. **YUK... That's disgusting!**

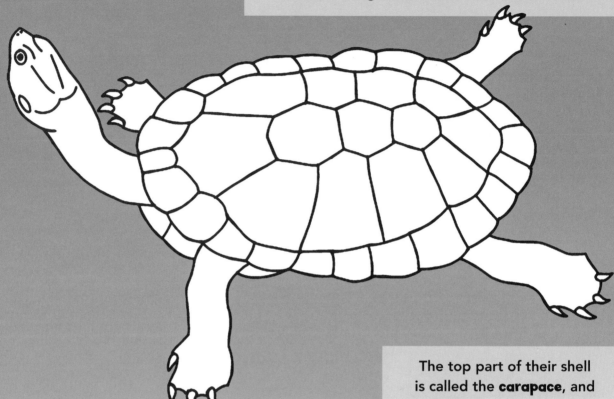

The top part of their shell is called the **carapace**, and the bottom part is called the **plastron**. All together it serves as great protection from attack by predators.

These turtles hunt for worms, insects, tadpoles, fish, yabbies and more. They are vital for the health of waterways because they consume dead organisms, which helps to prevent the water becoming polluted and deoxygenated. **They are nature's garbage collectors!**

The nose is at the top of the head, a bit like a built-in snorkel so that they can breathe as they swim beneath the water. Some Australian turtles can absorb oxygen through their bottom. **Who would have thought it? A bum-breathing turtle!**

SCAN HERE to watch a WILD clip

asozul

Saltwater Crocodile

Crocodylus porosus

WARNING: Don't be fooled by their name – they can travel great distances inland, residing in freshwater ecosystems as well. Do not swim in a crocodile's territory. You will end up as **LUNCH!**

They can have more than 60 teeth in their mouths, which fall out but are constantly replenished. Humans only get two sets of teeth in their lives, whereas crocodiles' teeth grow back again and again. **If there's a crocodile tooth fairy they'd be pretty busy!**

As adults, Saltwater Crocodiles are top-order **apex predators**, which means that they eat everything else. They can grow to more than **6 metres** in length.

They are ambush predators. Once their prey is taken, they'll drag their dinner down under the water and **'death-roll.'** Saltwater Crocodiles don't chew their food, and they swallow it in huge pieces.

SCAN HERE
to watch a WILD clip

egozic

Green Tree Frog
Litoria caerulea

Adult female

One female can lay up to 2,000 eggs, which hatch into tadpoles in three days, then gradually grow legs and turn into froglets and frogs over about six weeks.

They are long-lived amphibians and have been recorded to live for more than **40 years** in captivity.

Green Tree Frogs do not keep their eyes open whilst eating, and they use their eye-balls to assist in pushing large food items down their throat. **WOW WOW WOW!**

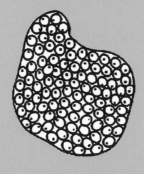

They are excellent climbers. The **adhesive discs** on their toes mean that they can even climb up glass. **Spiderman eat your heart out!**

These frogs do a great job for us – **they eat up all of the bugs.** They like to hang out near fluorescent lights at night, because these are very attractive to all manner of insects – **it's like a frog restaurant.**

Green Tree Frogs have glandular skin which can absorb moisture and oxygen – they can **drink through their skin like a sponge.**

Tadpoles

When attacked, Green Tree Frogs **can wee all over you like a frog water pistol...** in the hope that you don't eat them!

SCAN HERE
to watch a WILD clip

aviges

Juvenile frog

Tawny Frogmouth
Podargus strigoides

Tawny Frogmouths are **nocturnal** – they have large eyes for seeing in the dark. They eat insects, arthropods, small reptiles, small birds, and even frogs.

Tawny Frogmouths have a huge, wide, gaping gob to catch insects on the wing – **just like a huge net to trap their food!**

These birds have 'soft' feet for perching, and don't have large talons for grasping prey like owls do. Check out the **sensory feathers** on the top part of their head – these are for detecting bugs.

Tawny Frogmouths have powdery down feathers. They shed a fine waxy powder that acts as waterproofing. **No need to wear a rain jacket!**

For a relatively small bird they have an enormously **large beak**. To make sure that they don't topple over with the weight, the bottom part is made up of a frame with skin stretched across... kind of like a pelican's bill.

When breeding, Tawny Frogmouths lay their two or three eggs in the **flimsiest of nests**. They have a reputation for being a very bad nest-builder.

Eggs

Nestling

SCAN HERE
to watch a WILD clip

akesel

Barn Owl

Tyto alba

Barn Owls are best identified by their heart-shaped facial disc, which helps funnel sound towards their ears (just behind their eyes). Amazingly, the left ear is lower than the right, helping them to pinpoint exactly where their prey is located. **It's like 3D listening!**

This owl is known as a **'boom and bust' species**, and its breeding season is dependent on prey availability. They have the ability to produce multiple clutches of young when food is abundant.

They have 14 vertebrae in their necks – more than people – and they can spin their heads around 270°. **Like something in a horror movie!**

Chick

Barn Owls are commonly found in open spaces, including farmlands and forests with grassy understorey. Hunting and feeding at night, they prey on small mammals such as rodents, small possums, reptiles and amphibians.

Barn Owls are **silent hunters** of the night. Their incredibly soft feathers are uniquely structured and arranged, which allows air to pass over them soundlessly and absorbs most noise from their flapping wings.

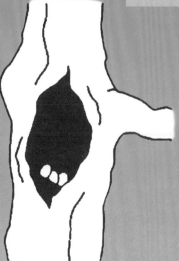

Tree Hollow Nest

SCAN HERE
to watch a WILD clip

ucerul

Laughing Kookaburra

Dacelo novaeguineae

Instantly recognisable, this iconic bird is Australia's largest **kingfisher** species, and has adapted to drier ecosystems, where it is a highly successful carnivorous hunter.

Laughing Kookaburras require dead hollows in trees for nest sites. In many suburban areas of Australia, loss of suitable nest sites has been the cause of local reductions in kookaburra populations. **We need to do more to help them out.**

Adult

The loud 'koo-koo-koo-koo-kaa-kaa-kaa-kaa' is often sung in chorus with other family members to ward off competitors and other species from the territory. **Basically saying, BACK OFF... if you come into our territory, you'll pay the price!**

The kookaburra often calls to welcome the dawn in the morning and sunset in the evening. It is quite possibly **the most famous sound in the Australian bush.**

Offspring from the previous breeding season **help their parents** to raise the next clutch of chicks. Juvenile kookaburras can be distinguished from adults as they have smaller beaks.

Once caught, kookaburras violently **BASH** their prey against a tree branch to kill their victim, whether it's an insect, a small bird or lizard, a worm, or **even a sausage** stolen from a barbecue!

Chick

Nest

Juvenile

SCAN HERE
to watch a WILD clip

ucomar

Short-beaked Echidna
Tachyglossus aculeatus

Echidnas are **a real success story**, being Australia's most widespread naturally occurring mammal, found in a diverse range of habitats and environments. They walk with a distinctive waddling gait and are surprisingly efficient climbers and swimmers.

Incredibly, the tip of their tongue can bend into a U-shape to reach around corners inside ant and termite colonies. Echidnas have been known to lick up 200 grams of ants in ten minutes. **That's like a built-in vacuum cleaner!**

These distinctive mammals are **monotremes**, and are the closest living relative of the Platypus. The female echidna lays one **leathery egg**, which is placed in a rudimentary pouch on her underbelly and takes only 10 days to hatch. A baby echidna is known as a **puggle**.

Puggle

Echidnas are curious animals as their front feet face forwards and their back feet face backwards. They can dig down directly beneath themselves, in order to avoid danger and predation. **Just like an earthworks excavator!**

SCAN HERE
to watch a WILD clip

okohil

Western Grey Kangaroo

Macropus fuliginosus

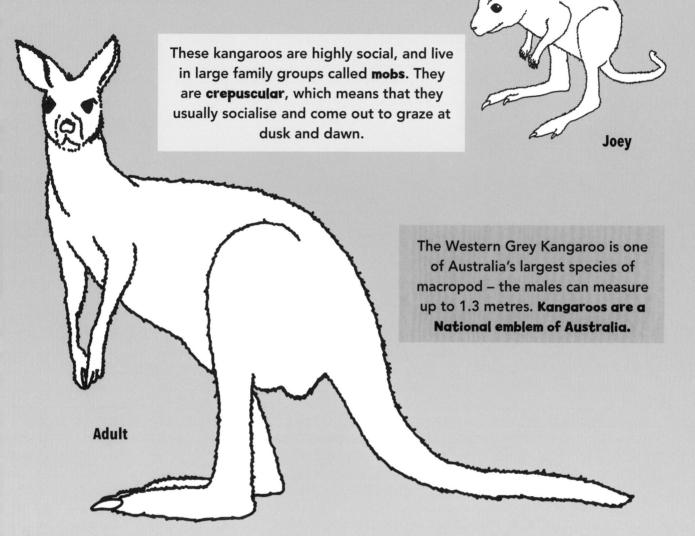

These kangaroos are highly social, and live in large family groups called **mobs**. They are **crepuscular**, which means that they usually socialise and come out to graze at dusk and dawn.

Joey

Adult

The Western Grey Kangaroo is one of Australia's largest species of macropod – the males can measure up to 1.3 metres. **Kangaroos are a National emblem of Australia.**

They are masters of survival in harsh landscapes and can exist on nutrient-poor foods such as grass. They are generally herbivorous, but have been recorded eating carrion (dead flesh) to supplement their diets with protein. **Who would have thought!**

Kangaroos employ **pentapedal** locomotion, employing all limbs and their huge tail to assist in forward motion. They can reach speeds of up to 64km per hour. **Their long tail is like a 'tight-rope' pole** for balance and changing direction.

SCAN HERE
to watch a WILD clip

apajus

Koala

Phascolarctos cinereus

It is the male Koala that usually **bellows** deeply. This guttural sound can be quite terrifying to the uninitiated. The noise they make is famous in Aussie folklore.

Joey

Adult

These **endemic marsupials** have incredible adaptations for life in trees. They have strong muscular limbs with powerful claws, and two opposable thumbs for gripping onto branches and tree trunks.

The joey Koala must inoculate itself with bacteria, which enable it to digest toxic gum leaves, **by eating its mother's poo!** This behaviour is called coprophagia.

When born, the joey Koala is the size of a **jelly bean**. It crawls into its mother's backward-facing pouch and stays there for up to seven months.

It is thought that less than 80,000 wild Koalas remain in their natural environment. Scientists predict that wild Koalas could become **extinct by 2050**.

Koalas can eat up to 1kg of gum leaves a day. These are very poor in nutritional value so a koala must **sleep up to 20 hours a day** to efficiently digest its food.

SCAN HERE
to watch a WILD clip

iwodot

Grey-headed Flying-fox

Pteropus poliocephalus

This is the largest bat in Australia – it can have a wingspan of up to one metre when outstretched. The common name of 'flying-fox' refers to the canine-like appearance of the head.

When flying-foxes have parasites such as lice, they don't need medicated shampoos from the chemist – they simply hang upside-down and wee on themselves. The uric acid in their urine eradicates the itchy unwelcome pests. **What a clever idea!**

Unlike small insectivorous bats, flying-foxes do not use echolocation – instead they have large eyes enabling them to see well in the dark, and they have an **excellent sense of smell**.

This species is listed as a **vulnerable to extinction**. Its population is rapidly declining due to loss of habitat, climate change and persecution by humans.

These 'fruit bats' are a **keystone species**, and are one of the most important animals in Australia. As they fly around they poop out fruit seeds and help to revegetate the barren landscape. **They only eat fruit and pollen - they won't suck your blood!**

SCAN HERE
to watch a WILD clip

aboqor

Giant Burrowing Cockroach

Macropanesthia rhinoceros

These incredible arthropods are found only in tropical woodlands of Far North Queensland. They can grow up to the size of an adult human's hand. Their tunnels can be as long as 6m and as deep as 1m underground. They are **our environmental friend**.

Unfortunately, cockroaches have an image problem. But there are more than 4,600 different cockroach species around the world, and only four of them are considered pests. **The rest are just going about their jobs, keeping our natural world healthy!**

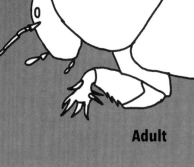

Nymphs

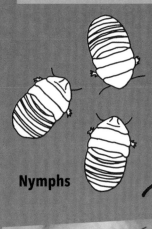

Adult

They emerge at night to gather food, which is the abundant fallen eucalyptus leaves on the forest floor. **For such a tiny animal it really does have such a HUGE job to do!** So many other plants and animals benefit from this amazing insect going about its business!

SCAN HERE
to watch a WILD clip

ikemic

Published in 2021 by Reed New Holland Publishers
Sydney • Auckland

Level 1, 178 Fox Valley Road, Wahroonga, NSW 2076, Australia
5/39 Woodside Avenue, Northcote, Auckland 0627, New Zealand

newhollandpublishers.com

Managing Director: Fiona Schultz
Publisher and Project Editor: Simon Papps
Designer: Andrew Davies
Production Director: Arlene Gippert

Printed in China
10 9 8 7 6 5 4 3 2 1

Also available from Reed New Holland:
Chris Humfrey's Awesome Australian Animals
ISBN 978 1 92554 670 5

For details of hundreds of other Natural History titles see www.newhollandpublishers.com

And keep up with Reed New Holland and New Holland Publishers

f ReedNewHolland

◎ @NewHollandPublishers and @ReedNewHolland